Stitching Porcelain

Stitching Porcelain

After Matteo Ricci
in Sixteenth-Century China

Deborah Larsen

A New Directions Book

Acknowledgments: Grateful acknowledgment is made to the editors and publishers of magazines and anthologies in which some of the poems—sometimes in different versions—in this collection first appeared: *Arvon International Poetry Competition 1987 Anthology* (Arvon Foundation, Great Britain); *The Gettysburg Review; The Nation; The Uncommon Touch* (a Stanford University Press anthology).

Manufactured in the United States of America
New Directions books are printed on acid-free paper
First published as New Directions Paperbook 710 in 1991
Published simultaneously in Canada by Penguin Books Canada Limited

Library of Congress Cataloging-in-Publication Data
Larsen, Deborah.
    Stitching porcelain : after Matteo Ricci in sixteenth-century
China / Deborah Larsen.
        p.   cm.
    ISBN 0–8112–1161–4
    1. Ricci, Matteo, 1552–1610—Poetry.   2. China—History—Ming
dynasty, 1368–1644—Poetry.   I. Title.
PS3562.A729S7   1991
811'.54—dc20   90–21176
                                                                   CIP

New Directions Books are published for James Laughlin
by New Directions Publishing Corporation,
80 Eighth Avenue, New York 10011

For Aimee

In Memory of

Anna Jacobs (Jakubíček) Maertz
Ralph Joseph Maertz
Consuelo Peil Maertz

Requiescant in actione

Contents

Preface

This sequence is based on the life of Matteo Ricci, the Italian Jesuit who settled in China in 1583 and who remained there until his death in 1610. I learned about Ricci in 1963 when as an undergraduate I took a Far East history course; I was immediately enamored of this courageous, canny man and of the country that was China. In 1985 I read Jonathan D. Spence's astonishing *The Memory Palace of Matteo Ricci* and this book rekindled for me the image of the strange, brilliant, sympathetic figure with whom I had been fascinated.

Matteo Ricci left a journal in which the writing is elegant and restrained; he also wrote letters. We know that he was born in Macerata, studied in Rome, sailed from Lisbon to India on the *St. Louis*, entered Canton in Buddhist dress, suffered losses on water and injury from robbers, made an awe-inspiring map, adopted the Mandarin hat-and-silks, prostrated himself before an empty Dragon Throne. This is the actual broad narrative line.

Umberto Eco has said that the ". . . author should die once he has finished writing. So as not to trouble the path of the text." This is good advice. But I would like the reader to know that I imagined some events, elaborated others, softened or omitted still others. Everywhere in the Ricci journals there was a sense of something afoot, unwritten.

—Deborah Larsen
Palo Alto, California /Gettysburg, Pennsylvania

While the day is cool
and the shadows are dispersing,
turn . . . and show yourself

  —The Song of Songs

I

Stitching Porcelain

You yield all the grains, the drifts
of winter wheat. You yield the grapevine,
lamb, oil of sesame, cinnamon, and palm.
You do not yield olives nor almonds:
I do not wish for almonds nor olives.
You yield sweet-tempered horses,
unshod, and no match for the Tartars':
my desire was never to fight the Tartars.
The Yangtze, the Yellow, and all the rivers
are dense with your fishes: I shudder
with them at night, dark gill to gill.
Although you yield no lions nor elephants,
in Peking I once caught sight
of an actual elephant—an astonishing importation.
Your porcelain is so fine, so thin,
a brass wire can repair it
to hold the new rice-wine.
Once I saw you beneath the bamboo
of a thousand facets—slim sticks,
nodes and joints—bent back

*Matteo Ricci meditates on the
Middle Kingdom's riches.*

from the world, stitching porcelain.
I write you a letter of praise
on your own fine cotton paper: I inscribe
all its fibers. My pleasure is in your tea,
your rhubarb, your lacquer, your ginger;
I sit down at the base of your cedar,
your casket-wood, the sign of mourning.
Here is a candle, rare wax, from the worms
you breed in trees: may its light fall
on hooves that never knew iron,
on no olives nor almonds,
on no indigenous elephants.

A Captain in His Pride: 1578

When I was titled Captain and went down to the sea,
to the port of Lisbon to muster my fine sailors,
those of our Portuguese navy, the finest on the waters,
the bells of the Church of the Wounds of Christ
began to toll, there was a parade in my name,
there were jugglers, long silk flags, flotillas
glittering for my pleasure in the sun.
    And when I drew close to that same sea,
so close I saw the ropes bundling firm the planks
of my carrack's stern, my fine sailors
proved *tailors, cobblers, lackeys, ploughmen,*
new recruits from the countryside, and I in my
pride, then, had to teach them
port from starboard by tying great heads of garlic
on one side of the *Jesus* and long strings of onion on the other.
      And after I put out on that same sea,
it was then I was blown backward two days' running
off the Cape of Storms, it was then the green timbers
gave up their nails, then that the keel wood
split and the astrolabes stuck, then that all our bile
turned the shadowed decks slick and shining and I became captain.

A captain around the time of Matteo's sailing reflects on his commission.

At the Equator on Board
the Carrack St. Louis

Matteo writes to his friend,
historian Gian Pietro Maffei,
from shipboard on the long
1578 sea voyage from Lisbon
to Goa.

Gian Pietro, if you receive the words of this letter,
praise God the Father of all for the miracle.
The novitiate—basin, pitcher, and smooth
pine pallet—never prepared me for this.
The worst is that the ink dries up in the heat:
words disappear from our pages like anchors hauled
from the sea floor, like traitors released to a mob.
A word floats away like a pilot's thumb
severed after blistering choices
during some Cimmerian storm. The setting down
of words is here stalked by a white-hot shade.
These words are like dried hairs curling up
from St. Gerasina's shrunken head, a woody
nest which we held aloft in processions
around the swaying deck: our sighing
intercession for continued winds.
What words give, what words take away,
what the significance of saying
"that which I have written,
I have not written."

Gian Pietro, I remember
how once at noon in our cloistered
Roman gardens, a three-band golden bee
passed into a blue droning of tuberose,
how, once, a blackbird threw no shadow.

Under a Brown Sail

Macao to Canton: 1583

That day under a brown sail we crowded north
against the verges of delta, edges of river.
The ginger, cassia, cane grew black
in dropping light until a flash
of white sturgeon became the very link
to the astrobodies of night:
we had entered the Grand Silence of a great swarm.

Ruggieri and I had an appointment with the Middle Kingdom,
we were wearing the wigs of the shorn, the masks
of new beardlessness. That night we sailed freely,
unrecognized, past the shored watchman's sibylline drumming.

*Matteo and a companion,
Michele Ruggieri, set out by
junk from Macao. It is
September. They have adopted
Buddhist dress and have
shaven their heads and their
beards: they hope, in this
fashion, to be viewed by the
Chinese as monks.*

The Plateau

There was lightning last evening and a little rain.
This morning, sun touches the edge of the cassia-flower.
Nothing is falling. A small stream continues through the middle
of the plain beyond the tower and the land heaps up with vegetables.
Orchards rise from the hills in shapely plantings:
triangles of grape, trapezoids of orange, squares of Persian apple.

In isolation here a holy man once lived,
pounding and sifting rice all day. He imposed the austerity
of iron chains against his flesh so that rounded
wounds appeared and filled with maggots at the waist,
the wrists, and the ankles.
What did he care for the divided plateau?

A legendary holy man, a Buddhist, had once lived on a lush plateau which Matteo now visits.

When one of these maggots dropped off, this man would say,
"Why do you think to desert me? Can you find nothing to gnaw?"
Perhaps he, echoing the poet, also counselled the maggot

on that matter of falling prey to desire: whatever Brother Maggot did,
he should not go near a lovely woman; a mere nine yards' worth
of approach is over-much, enough to send lines running
through lacquer, split a plum, crack a tooth, or break a wheel.

The Map

"What a bad break!"
—Cavafy, "Dareios"

The Governor said, "Li, I have been thinking,
could you make your European map of the world speak Chinese?"
And so I set to work. A little annotation here,
Chinese characters there, clear as I can make them.
I dared to show China as only part of the great East,
but by omitting the first meridian of the Fortunate Islands
and then making margins, the Middle Kingdom
appeared, as the people here expected, right in the center.

*Matteo's map delighted many.
And then—invaders.*

It was as if I had scattered seeds for hungry birds:
the rough space that was our doorway actually grew larger
from the constant brush of bodies passing through it.
It was like the kisses smoothing Roman Peter's feet.
For years, palanquins crowded the streets about our house;
gondolas, nodding assent, bobbed on the river beyond the widening door.
Everyone said, "Look at the great stretch of land, of sea
between us and Europe." They said, "Why fear a people so far away?"

And then the news, an incredible interruption,
a threatened invasion by Japan, and what's more, fifteen thousand
of Hideyoshi's troops converted Christians. The plan:
they'd take Korea first and then on
to Peking to crush the emperor.
The emperor. By God, he was to be mine!
I was to convert him and all this country—I would have been
the new Paul, Chinese to the Chinese.

Now for fear of Christian foreigners
our doorway is dark and empty, the guó bird
droops in the cinnamon tree, our prism—an object
of wonder—hangs nearly opaque in the flat moonlight.
Now, in my sorrow, the western map that speaks Chinese
appears in this city at this hour
as a new and partly true
and oddly beautiful digression.

Changing Clothes:
From Buddhist to Mandarin

After Li Ho

I shuffle my robes: now I wear Mandarin dress.
My ankle-length silks smell of the rain.
The wind breathes up my Venetian-style sleeves.
Dusk is my purple belt, daybreak my high black hat.
    This branch with two cocoons is my crozier.
    Now in glittering slippers
    I wind my way up from the south;
    I stop the men from the north:
    Ho, you men shall soon eat sturgeon gills.
    But I shall eat moose nose.
Today I blossom out of the rough cloth of the Buddhist,
Tomorrow with silkworm casings grow ancient.

II

Mandarin

Now I know why you walk that way,
canted back, amphibious, set for the take-off,
approach, and new landing.
Because of your hat!—its ovate wings
so lightly attached to the black fabric
above your ears—a sign of your rank;
of your dignity; of the huge bones
in your wrist absorbing the shock,
vibrating across some throttle.

*The mandarin hat had
wing-like ovals attached so
tenuously to the fabric that one
had to stand erect to prevent
these adornments from falling
off.*

Two Poems of Nanking

Arrived at Nanking

The spirit here is gay, *hoi-polloi*, as well as solemn, the *lettered aristocracy*.
You are full of circling moats with water which itself circulates.
Your arched and twelve-gated second wall is about eighteen miles
in Italian measure.
If one rider, in fine spirits, started at the top of you,
and another smiling rider at the foot, and rode toward each other,
it would take a whole day for them, delighted, to come together.

In the fast boat from Nanking: prolepsis

At the first sight of the Yellow River,
its source beyond this silt and the borders of the kingdom
in the Lake of Constellations,
we shuddered with the cavalier galley
until the red lacquer on your nails cracked,
until I saw my own body
a notch, a white edge of splitting red,
and shooting ahead on the stream,
already an arrow on the Peking air.

The Loss of João Barradas
to the River Gan

Matteo's beloved traveling companion is swept away from the capsized cargo boat at "The Place of Eighteen Currents." João's body is never found.

A shudder, yesterday's sunlit deck atilt,
white water takes him by the nape beyond boards,
threads him struggling through the rapids
to a dusky afternoon at her loosening breast.
Now his lungs fill nearly smoothly
and bones, veins start coming unstrung.
He sinks, finally, to the waxing water's belly.

A pearly fish there senses something amazing and stays,
steadies itself near João's eye and arches slightly
its tiny radiant spine, lifts its flanking gills,
draws up, reins-in its open carriage for him,
attends his leggy being back-flowing the sluice.

Seals

I am opening the cabinet of this desk
and I am taking out the seals.
I am removing the wooden seals;
I am taking out the seal of marble
and the ones of ivory
and vermilion coral, names,
degrees and titles, the vows I would point to.
And I am taking away the use of the seals
for the stamping of objects.
Further, I am rubbing away
the imprints of the seals:
I am bleaching out characters;
removing them from old poems,
removing them from journals
bent on containing stray columns
of cloud and of fire,
removing them from sketches
that show only
the backs of male torsos.
                          And I am setting
you—*strong as death*, relentless
as gratitude—here instead, here
and here on my arm.

The Haft: Ricci in Thought

Retelling Meng Chiao's Stone Bridge Mountain Poem

I make my way alone on this path,
a simple weight in my hand—my axe.
The haft has weathered, forking with age.
I have been so long in thought
I lose a sense of edges:
the blade of my gnarled forefinger flashes.
Even that stone bridge is more than its span.

Looking at the Empty Dragon Throne

1

I passed through frost and under stars
but the *only moving thing*
was the empty Dragon Throne.

2

I was single-minded
like cedar branches
which when laced can form a footstool or a throne.

3

I kowtowed before the whirling throne
in ritual red damask and clanking helmet.

*After twenty years in China,
Matteo is at last summoned to
audience with the Emperor. But
Wanli does not appear and
Matteo prostrates himself before
an empty Dragon Throne.*

4

Here
there were eunuchs
and men
and a throne.

5

Surely the Emperor
would at least appear
behind his slatted blind
from the balcony set just above
the whistling throne.

6

But his shadow never darkened
the screen behind the throne
raised between four columns
at the top of marble stairs.
Nor could I catch the glintings
of icy greens and sapphires;
those coronal, frontal pendants.

7

O imagine how it sounded
when I shouted the tribute,
"Ten thousand years!"
and it echoed back to me
and it echoed off the hollow-footed throne:

8

I was wormwood and no man.
A void moved, and I vomited
a projectile of blood, fire, hail,
scalding stars which wheeled:
was I the Lunatic of Thronal Delusions?

9

I had borne a flame from Macerata.
I had circled this Forbidden City
to attain a bitter throne, a gall.

10

I kept the seven thunderclaps of my anger secret;
I did not cry them out before the throne.
For had I not sunk my right foot in foreign soil?
My left foot had I not already vested in the sea?

11

I rode horseback, carrack, cart;
and now this green,
sour taste rides me.
Now I know
the devastation of concubines
cut off by conversions from all the little thrones.

12

Nothing is moving.
The throne is in stasis. Can an arrow fly?

13

O innocent payers of tribute, leave
the Throne Hall of Assured Peace with me.
Shoot out
the Gates of Supreme Harmony even as
the imagined world sinks in the sockets of afternoon.

14

Then out on the road
(with the earth opening up),
act to remember, in second innocence,
the first persons you see.
Enthrone them in your mind's eye:
two persons—one thin and poor, the other
fat and precarious
as a herd of sheep or spreading stain.

A Natural History

Above forked roots the blossom simply opens
and then withers to the quick, a nub of gourd
which is slipped inside a clay or wooden casing
so that the fruit will push toward general shape
and take the impress of particularities,
tiny ideograms and mythic grins cut
in the cave-like inner surface of the mold.
One morning we found these artifices,
like slim-waisted girls, at vines' ends in the sun
all over our host's garden floor.
Then the grown and ripened flesh
is hollowed, dried, and readied
for a lath-work top of rosewood or of bonewood.

    This is the simple history
of a chamber for the cricket
who once inside his house and carried close
against a person's chest, the lattice of a heart;
or fed some specks of pure white radish,
grows wild to vocalize and sings
and sings so that the cage
threatens to seed and flower again,
again and again as his bounds
set him down in the decorous, slatted dark.

Hearing Confession

The physicians say the ancients said
that in the presence of a terrified woman,
the empathic man may feel stirrings:
nightcrawlers criss-crossing the polished floors
of the vault of his groin.
But behind this screen in the house of a new convert
as I hear a wife's gasping confession
it is my heart which goes out to her
and I struggle to keep myself
for both of us, breathing.

New Litany for the Disguised Brother Benedetto de Goís as He Begins the Overland Journey to Cathay, 1603

Was there a "Cathay" distinct from China? Benedetto de Goís sets out overland to find out. Matteo, in Peking, and near the end of his life, hears of this journey and prays for the traveler.

1

Consider him.
At the first drum roll before dawn, may he pack away his tent
speedily;
At the second roll, may he properly load his camel;
At the third roll, may he mount his camel day after day.
In the traversing of the first glacier, consider him.
In a descent into the second gorge, consider.
In the peeling and splitting open of his cheeks and in their
bleedings,
Consider him.

2

O Lord, where are you! Out giving the hawk advice?
Consider him.
He will lose fistfuls of hair at Attock-on-Indus.
He will retch with the swaying of camels,
He will not gauge the third minor cleft before the Pass of Parwan,
The labyrinths of his ears will deceive him.
He will walk backwards when he hears a flute and a lyre,
He will wander two days among the pistachio bushes.
O Lord, where are you! Out feeding squab?

3

Look after him.
O Lord, where are you! Out endowing the cock with foreknowledge?
Consider him.
In his dropping wild cherries in water to ward off the flux,
In his forgetting Lahore, where he started,
In his fumbling the scimitar, bow, and quiver,
In his longings to wear his soutane again,
In the swellings of his gums and groin,
In his gorging himself on the white-fleshed melons of Hami,
Look after him.

4

Teach him to use his wits.
Look after him.
O Lord, where are you! Out making your voice carry?
Consider him.
When he disentangles himself from the spindled legs
 of the gryphon-fighting storks and afterwards says long prayers
  in the night, tell him to stop it and get to sleep.
Where diamonds grow like hazelnuts, let him pick in moderation.
In like manner, let him comb only the silk he needs from the cedar.
Let him refuse to allow a thin lynx to stare at the soles of his shoes.
Teach him to use his wits.

5

Lead him inside himself and back out.
Teach him to use his wits.
Look after him.
O Lord, where are you! Out meeting with the janitors of Sheol?
Consider him.
Lead him from the Ravine of Baboons to the Eastern Gobi.
May he not sing the *Nunc dimittis* prematurely.
May he recognize the Roof of the World when he sees it.
May he catch sight of the Great Wall from afar
    and give the vision of it back for generations
        after resting briefly in its suns and shadows.
Lead him inside himself and back out.

The Ruined Concubine:
Complaint Against the Jesuit Ricci

After Meng Chiao

A curse on you, Far Westerner.
You have sundered me from my lord;
he has put me away.
Once we were joined under heaven:
again and again I lay with him;
a gentle, a courteous, and a humorous man.

Even as I moved quietly about
in brilliant mornings
enjoying memorious edgings,
the traceries of night;
already you were sailing eastward,
your black ship's monstrous canvas
flapping toward us like the shadowed wings
on some bent-necked stork.

Recalling Former Travels # 4

After Tu-Mu

This East-and-West-of-the-Waters Abbey,
sycamore, old hills, *wind in the upper rooms*—
Between sober and sober I concentrated three days
while the white cows turned grey at their grazings
against the openings in the blossoming snow.

III

> *But it rides time like riding a river. . . .*
> *—"The Wreck of the Deutschland"*

1

O God, this boat—
this cod's head, mackerel tail;
this beamy, crosstreed bark
hull-downing in fore winds—
help. By the fixed-and-flashing light
I would tack the zigzag course
right upwind and into the straits
so that I sing this history's coming about.

Matteo Ricci, on his deathbed, reflects.

2

On May the third
I took off my embroidered slippers
and stepped up to the loose-bricked bed
of my death. Mollie, O
Mollymawk, O littlest, ghosty albatross,
attend me here in these last nights
where the polyphon memory counters the plain
chantey of hoisting a heavy body heavenward.

3

Sloping ledges,
Macerata of cypresses,
an infant's scalp skin mottles
against the grey blade of the womb.
Was I the child, rolling soft
in amnion, Giovan's, Giovanna's,
grandson of dear Luria,
heart's thimble, little nudge, blue as a hedgehog?

4

And did this feathery
flesh age and skew—wrenched ankle,
twisted heel—in an eastern garden
when robbers broke upon us
and my very student rebuked my restraint?
Take away my fingered scrip and compass,
take away my vain staff.
Let mortal sprains recount the weather.

5

I was the child.
Tutored by Nicoló and so grew
to love the Rome of buckling arches,
hanks of hair, pieces of bone,
where the vault was void in an erotic sky,
where watery lights appeared to anchor dusk
and a woman in ankle bells unveiled
a breast so full it drove a Cardinal wild.

6

The veiled the more sublime.
At the place of Eighteen Currents
where I later lost Barradas, I rescued
a slim-waisted consort who revealed nothing
but shock at my exotic foreign face:
white water, her terror, my face; under wet silk,
that waist, my terror, her grace—*let
Me live to my sad self hereafter kind.*

7

Caught, ageing, *in that*
sensual music, I later could
more skillfully chart land, the seas:
cartography—that clear, bound
line—is no country for the young.
Who makes an artifice of temporality
stands the firestorms of eros,
chooses, and then may make a map—

8

So place a note
off the coast of Goa,
a word on the verge of Macao,
a character clear
as crystal near the silver mines
at Potosí: let the marginal speak
to that slant passage,
those spaces called shoals in the charts of the known.

9

When it came time
to annotate my map
near Mozambique, I remembered
black faces flattened
in grief: slaves being loaded and loaded
on the *Good Jesus,* the *St. Gregory,*
and my own *St. Louis;* until, with weight,
the ships' dark strakes dropped under the waterline.

10

As now I feel
a dropping away: with such freight
gathering below, glossed body-hoops may well
fault and buckle, water dampen
the weevils in their biscuits while our baboon-watch
startles in the shrouds; what we at first
will think of as evil, an auster, will blow;
will force us kindly close to the common-ribbed keel.

11

Some find that hair-thin
bloodline rising beneath
the press of a blade a sign, a lamp,
a bugle to our dimness;
I remember when the whale, that grampus,
blew: the sailors on the *St. Louis*
loved to say it was the cold spout they'd
bucketed to rouse the sleeping watchman from his sins.

12

So some days
here my heart jumped land:
I longed to ship to the young
stones of an Italian coast and sit
shadowed under a yellow gourd. But what, Lord,
if without me this people should wither as we know
the gourd would wither. In addition,
I saw a giant, hinge-jawed fish-mouth open—and I stayed.

13

In mid-July, like an arrow
Peking-northward-bound,
I sailed from Nanking in a fast boat
lent by a friend—reluctant,
frowning, but fearing offense. A fragrance!
when I stepped onto that light-boat: surely such odor
was symbol and sign of the holy?
It was fruit of arbutus, *gianmui,* the merest of cargo.

14

Then weight tutored
me; rank fruit in time
tamped down, on that canal, my manic spirit.
Nudewood, what was the lightest
of boats, lumbered through lock after lock;
was constantly tracked by men at ropes'-ends
who staggered on the diagonal
to counter that combing, the lateral mining of water.

15

I did not at first give thought
to, call Christ to this,
nor myself Cyrene to a nightmare
of scabrous bodies hauling my load;
their shoulder-welts, their cross-etched flesh
from hard daylight knifing through woven hats
dimmed me. God! I thought in panic, how else
might I have gotten up these locks?

16

They loom there . . .
These are the pied men,
the men brindled as Roman flagellants
on Maundy Thursday. They move us
up the tumid water. Their backs are firewalkers'
feet; their backs are dappled landscapes, graphs,
quilts, ploughed fields, and cracking clay.
Their hooded, staring eyes are everywhere.

17

Our heart-valves
sough, hesitate, and seal, becoming
instruments of narrow music.
I grow thin on this canal, a form
undone by feldspar, air, and star.
Cast me as an antique server: I'd play to backs
to wake a blank Wanli, the eunuchs,
mandarins; and Her whom, not possessing, my heart loves.

On Hearing of Matteo Ricci's Death:
The Rescued Consort's Song

She saw the Far Westerner only once
but she is singing his spirit lifted apart,
for a time, from what we knew as his body.

She is singing of density, of his soul now
as strung and his huge body unstrung
as the loose lappings of sea.

She always imagined his spirit fibrous as sailfish
and his body a watery tacking;
in a monotone wave she saw

one of his thoughts as a bright sturgeon;
in the shallows a compassionate act
showed itself velvety as a bat-ray.

His look of love appeared to her as a sharp-edged,
scalloped shell in a chancy surf
filmy as her own veil or a looking-glass.

As the Preface indicates, Jonathan D. Spence's *The Memory Palace of Matteo Ricci* revived my longtime interest in Ricci. I drew many details, incidents, speeches, and images from Spence as well as from Vincent Cronin's *The Wise Man from the West* and from a version of Ricci's journals written by Nicola Trigault, S.J., translated by Louis J. Gallagher, S.J.: *China in the Sixteenth-Century: The Journals of Matthew Ricci* (this latter is really a kind of adaptation of Ricci's own *Historia* which in turn can be found as part of a larger work, *Fonti Ricciane*, edited by Pasquale D'Elia, S.J.). I have revised forward some poems from *Poems of the Late T'ang* (ed. by A. C. Graham). Italics (except where they indicate foreign words) in the body of a poem mean that a line or phrase is a quotation. Finally, Robert Alter described the work about which I continue to dream when he wrote that in the "ancient Near East a 'book' remained for a long time a relatively open structure."

A Captain in His Pride
The tailors and cobblers are reported by Spence as coming from one historian's "portmanteau listing" of new sailors.

The Plateau
The poet who gives counsel is Meng Chiao ("Impromptu" in *Poems of the Late T'ang*).

Mandarin
"Mandarin" is dedicated to Steven Rubey.

Looking at the Empty Dragon Throne
The image of the fat person is taken from Edward Schillebeeckx's wonderful discussion of the issue—in Ezekiel—of "fat" sheep not being forgotten nor "left in the lurch" (*God Among Us: The Gospel Proclaimed*).

A Natural History
Niceties about the growing of such gourds are drawn from a 1988 *New York Times* article by Orville Schell, "Foreign Affairs: Songs from Old China."

Hearing Confession
See "Hendrick's assertion"—enlarged in "Hearing Confession"—in Leston Havens' *Making Contact: The Uses of Language in Psychotherapy.*

Blue Lights
Blue lights—an antique system of signaling with flashes in patterns—occur when shipboard guns are fired at night.

Acknowledgments

I wish to thank Stanford University and its creative writing faculty for the Wallace Stegner Fellowship, and the Pennsylvania Council on the Arts for a Fellowship in Literature. I am especially grateful to Jonathan D. Spence whose work on Ricci has been an inspiration and a blessing. Many friends and relatives were supportive over the years as were some acquaintances who are writers of stature: I hope they will accept this collective mention of gratitude. My students and my colleagues at Gettysburg College continue to be a sustaining force.